Our Oregon

George Ostertag

Voyageur Press

First published in 2007 by Voyageur Press, an imprint of MBI Publishing Company, Galtier Plaza, Suite 200, 380 Jackson Street, St. Paul, MN 55101 USA

Editor: Josh Leventhal
Designer: Jennifer Bergstrom

Printed in China

Library of Congress Cataloging-in-Publication Data

Ostertag, George, 1957–
  Our Oregon / by George Ostertag.
    p. cm.
  ISBN-13: 978-0-7603-2921-4 (plc w/ jacket)
  ISBN-10: 0-7603-2921-4 (plc w/ jacket) 1. Oregon—
Pictorial works. 2. Oregon—History, Local—Pictorial works.
3. Oregon—Social life and customs—Pictorial works. 4.
Natural history—Oregon—Pictorial works. I. Title.
  F877.O78 2007
  979.5—dc22
                  2006034495

ON THE FRONT COVER

Mount Hood is the standout feature of the Oregon Cascades and, for many Oregonians, a state symbol.

ON THE SPINE

The Pacific rhododendron is a common but showy shrub in the Cascades forest.

ON THE BACK COVER

Top: Warm Springs Falls spills over a columnar basalt cliff in a secluded spot in Umpqua National Forest. *Middle:* The wildflowers of Jefferson Park shape a lovely foreground for Mount Jefferson. *Bottom Left:* In Oswald West State Park, the setting sun bathes Short Sand Beach in a wash of orange and pink. *Bottom Right:* Wildflowers and yellow roses adorn the historic Chandler Cabin, which now sits in the 1880s Park in Haines.

PAGE 1

In the Coast Range, in Siuslaw National Forest, picturesque Rock Creek threads through Rock Creek Wilderness.

PAGE 2

Near Coos Bay, a light has guided mariners at Cape Arago since 1866. The present light is the third one to occupy this site.

PAGE 3

A volcano within a volcano, Crater Lake's Wizard Island towers 764 feet above the famous lake's surface.

PAGE 4

Paulina Peak graces the crown of Newberry Volcano, Oregon's largest, but less well-known volcano.

PAGE 5, TOP

The International Rose Test Garden, with nearly ten thousand rose bushes, is a trademark of Portland, the "City of Roses."

PAGE 5, BOTTOM

A familiar feature of Portland's Willamette River skyline is the "Made in Oregon" sign, seen here from Eastside Esplanade.

ON THE TITLE PAGE

The Oregon Cascades are a four-season recreational playground; seen here is the snowy forest realm around Mount Washington.

ON THE TITLE PAGE, INSET

On the Three Capes Scenic Loop, Cape Meares Lighthouse, built in 1890, is one of nine remaining lighthouses on the Oregon coast.

Stretched along twelve miles of the southern Oregon coast, Samuel Boardman State Park serves up striking coastal views, including this one from Arch Rock Viewpoint. Offshore rocks along the Oregon shore are part of Oregon Islands National Wildlife Refuge.

ABOVE

Heceta Head Lighthouse is an icon of the Oregon coast
and the most photographed lighthouse in the state.
At Heceta Head Lightstation, the lightkeeper's house now
doubles as an interpretive center and a bed and breakfast.

LEFT

Rugged headland cliffs plunge to the sea, shaping this
dramatic shoreline along the central coast near Heceta
Head. Storm-shaped Sitka spruce trees often top the cliffs.

Parrot and Conical Rocks accentuate the walk to Heceta Head Lighthouse, north of Florence. Oregon has one of the highest-energy coasts in the world, with pounding surf and big storms. The clash of rock and sea is a breathtaking spectacle.

The state's 350-mile coastline includes beaches suitable for sunset strolls and horseback rides. Uninterrupted sandy strands allow visitors to find lonesome moments at the coast. Here, riders explore the beach at Bayocean Peninsula, site of an ambitious, but ill-thought-out, coastal town in the 1900s.

Oregon is a sunset coast. Here, the setting sun casts a golden glow over the cliffs at Cape Lookout State Park. This popular park outside Tillamook offers a five-mile spit for beach strolls and a headland promontory for hiking and whale watching.

ABOVE

Gulls are a signature of the Oregon coast and delight onlookers, despite being a common fixture. Gulls nest along the coastal cliffs and on the offshore rocks. They can be spied bathing in the freshwater streams, robbing unattended picnic baskets, or gorging on sand crabs.

RIGHT

Beachcombers delight in subtle finds of agates, shells, and glass floats along Oregon's shores; sometimes they are treated to a live encounter, such as this Dungeness crab that has wandered ashore. The delectable crab is highly sought after by commercial and recreational crabbers. For many Oregon coast visitors, crabbing, clamming, and surf fishing are primary pursuits.

Sea lions are the more gregarious members of the pinniped (fin-footed) family. They can be distinguished from harbor seals by their overall size, ears, and barking. Sea lions gather at docks and bays and on offshore rocks suitable for sunning.

Beachcombing sometimes results in a rare find. This blacktail deer was discovered at low tide, hiding in a sea cave in the cliffs at Cape Lookout. Footprints are more common proof that wildlife species share the beach. Because high tide poses a danger to wildlife, the deer's time in the cave was short term, traded for the more dependable forest cover.

Oregon Dunes National Recreation Area stretches nearly fifty miles between Florence and Coos Bay. Origin of the dunes traces back 7,000 years, and wind continues to finesse the landscape, sculpting dunes up to 400 feet tall. Plants require stubborn resilience to gain a niche in this ever-shifting landscape.

The shifting sands of the dunes trap freshwater, forming lakes, critical for wildlife. Here, a great blue heron probes the edge of Tahkenitch Lake in search of food. Birdwatchers enjoy a variety of sightings in the forest, dune, lake, estuary, and shore habitats of Oregon Dunes National Recreation Area.

BELOW

Pacific rhododendron is prolific in Oregon, decorating both the shore and the mountains of the Coast and Cascade Ranges. The coastal bloom launches the show, and each May, Florence hosts the Rhododendron Festival. These particular blooms decorate the slope of Elbow Lake in Oregon Dunes National Recreation Area.

Situated where the Columbia River empties into the Pacific Ocean, the town of Astoria includes a collection of notable Victorian homes. The Flavel House was built in 1885 for Captain George Flavel, a successful Columbia River bar pilot. The Queen Anne-style home has been restored to its original elegance and now houses a fine museum. From the fourth-floor cupola, Captain Flavel kept watch over the river bar activity.

Above Astoria, atop Coxcomb Hill, rises this 125-foot stately column wrapped in the area's history. It records the story of the Native Americans, the early explorers, and John Jacob Astor, Astoria's namesake. A climb of the column's 164 stairs leads to the balcony and a view of the coast, Coast Range, and distant Cascades.

Yaquina Bay Bridge in Newport cuts a striking sunrise image. Many of the spans along the Oregon coast, including this one, were the vision of Conde B. McCullough, master bridge builder. His concept for bridge design combined aesthetics with function, and the bridges are civil engineering landmarks. McCullough bridges often include soaring arches, dignified gateway spires, and architectural railings.

As seen here from the Yaquina Bay Bridge, the Newport waterfront remains a busy hub for commercial and recreational boating.

Commercial fishing is part of the romance of the coast, but it doesn't come without inherent risk. This Fisherman's Memorial, honoring this seafaring legacy, is at the marina in Charleston.

This rickety old structure on Youngs Bay speaks of more productive days on the Astoria waterfront. Fishing fleets and canneries were an integral part of the town's early economy.

Carnival lights brighten the evening sky at the Rhododendron Festival in Florence, and the Siuslaw River holds a shimmering liquid double of the fanfare. Oregon's calendar year is chock-full of festivals, events, and fairs, keeping carnivals crisscrossing the state.

On the coast near North Bend and Coos Bay, Shore Acres State Park rolls out an enchanting seven-acre formal garden beneath the native Sitka spruce trees; shown here are the Garden House and fountain. The park occupies the former estate of Louis B. Simpson, the pioneer shipping-and-timber magnate who planted the original garden.

Viewed from Pittock Mansion high in Portland's West Hills, Mount Hood looms above the city and surrounding countryside. Pittock Mansion is one of many attractions along the Wildwood Trail, a popular West Hills trail serving hikers, joggers, and casual strollers.

ABOVE

The repeating arches of the Rogue River Bridge disappear into the summer fog at Gold Beach. Temperature inversions occur when the inland valley temperatures soar. The hot air rises, pulling in the cool coastal air and fog.

Rose Festival fireworks light up the sky over the Willamette River and the Portland city skyline. In the "City of Roses," the Rose Festival jam-packs the June calendar with celebration. The festival has delighted Portlanders and city visitors for 100 years. The Grand Floral Parade, Fleet Week, the Starlight Parade, and the dragon boat races are other festival favorites.

Synchronized human power fuels this colorful dragon boat on the Willamette River. Portland has several active dragon boat teams, and practice sessions increase leading up to the Rose Festival dragon boat races in June. Scholars trace dragon boat racing back 2,500 years to south-central China, on the Yangtze River.

Portland's Tom McCall Waterfront Park is the city's playground; its Willamette River walk attracts cyclists, walkers, and joggers. Active Portlanders can fashion a variety of loops off the walk via the city's rich network of bridges and the popular Eastside Esplanade, the park's counterpart on the other side of the river.

Children delight in the cool refreshment of the Salmon Springs Fountain in Tom McCall Waterfront Park. This fountain cycles through a sequence of patterns, providing youngsters with a frequently changing playground.

Pioneer Courthouse Square, an important center for gathering and celebration, marks off the seasons in Portland. Here, the familiar umbrella-toting *Allow Me* statue shares the nighttime stage with the city's Christmas tree.

An autumn-gilded backdrop brings added poignancy to *The Promised Land* statue at Chapman Square in Portland's Plaza Blocks. Created by artist David Manuel, this bronze rendering of a pioneer family was commissioned by the Oregon Trail Coordinating Council to celebrate the 150th anniversary of the Oregon Trail in 1993.

Barber Block represents a restoration success story, preserving the city's historical architecture. On the National Register of Historic Places, this 1889 Victorian structure is one of East Portland's earliest commercial buildings. Extensive historical research helped restorers replicate the building's original exterior detail and paint color.

Portland's Saturday Market is held under the Burnside Bridge in Historic Old Town—on Saturdays *and* Sundays—bringing together crafters, food vendors, and street performers. This eye-catching performer in period garb fills the market air with the mystical notes of a European Dudelsack, an ancient instrument and forerunner to the contemporary bagpipe.

LEFT

A pair of ornate lions guards the gate at the entrance to Chinatown in Portland's Old Town District. Chinese restaurants, herb stores, Asian markets, and Portland's Classical Chinese Garden keep the spirit of this historical ethnic district alive.

BELOW

The Ballet Folklorico y Mariachi de Guadalajara performs Main Stage at the city's Cinco de Mayo Fiesta. The mariachi rhythms, the fast swirl of colorful skirts, and the traditional steps bridge the miles between Portland and her sister city Guadalajara, Mexico. Traditional food, information booths, carnival rides, and fireworks round out the celebration.

In 1917, as World War I raged across Europe, civic-minded Portlanders established the International Rose Test Garden in Washington Park to provide a safe haven for European hybrid roses. Portland's association with roses dates back to 1888, with the birth of its Rose Society. In 1905, the city's rose-bordered streets earned it the nickname "City of Roses."

Portland's Washington Park is home to one of the most authentic Japanese gardens outside of Japan. Designed by renowned authority Professor Takuma Tono, the five-and-a-half-acre Japanese Garden weaves a harmonious union of plant, stone, and water to cast a spell of tranquility. The influence of Shintoism, Taoism, and Buddhism is palpable in the simplicity, sculpture, and natural splendor.

LEFT

In a native forest setting, Portland's famous Hoyt Arboretum brings together a rich collection of more than one thousand trees and woody shrubs from around the world. A network of twelve miles of trail leads visitors through the living laboratory.

Henry Lewis Pittock, a newspaper magnate and astute businessman, was a leading figure in the burgeoning city of Portland in the early twentieth century. He and his wife, Georgiana, lived in this West Hills mansion from 1914 to 1919. The home, constructed of native materials by local craftsmen, shows an eclectic architecture, incorporating Turkish, French, and English influences. Its exquisite interior is seen by guided tour.

The steel suspension St. Johns Bridge, seen here from Cathedral Park, is one of Portland's loveliest Willamette River spans. The bridge stretches more than 2,000 feet in length and has twin Gothic towers. It was designed by the renowned American bridge engineer David Steinman. He selected its Verde green color to harmonize with the forest at the bridge's west end.

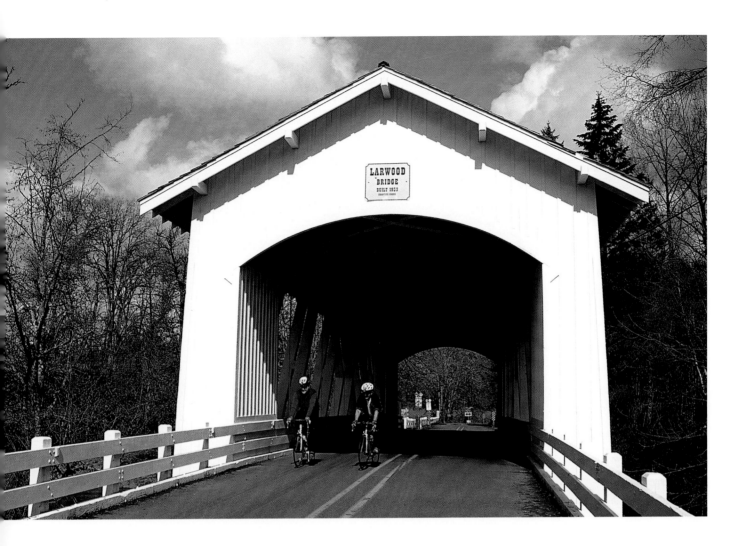

ABOVE

A more rustic-style bridge can be found near Albany in the Willamette River Valley. Larwood Bridge, spanning Crabtree Creek, is part of the region's Covered Bridge Country Tour. Oregon is one of a handful of states noted for its covered bridges, and the state's rural roads not only suggest scenic drives but welcome bicycle touring as well.

RIGHT

The lights of Christmas cheer decorate Woodburn's historic Settlemier House. Jesse Settlemier, the town founder, built this fourteen-room, Queen Anne and Craftsman–style Victorian mansion in 1892. Graceful parklike grounds and stately trees complement the grand dame. The home has been carefully restored by the French Prairie Historical Society and contains local artifacts.

The Philip Foster Farm National Historic Site, near Eagle Creek, rightfully claims a page in Oregon Trail history. Foster teamed with Sam Barlow to build the Barlow Trail, the Oregon Trail's overland bypass of Mount Hood. This wayside farm, with its store, cabins, meals, and fresh fruit, was a welcome sight for pioneers coming off the trail. Pioneer journals rhapsodize about arriving at Foster Farm and the first taste, literally and figuratively, of the journey's promise.

Atop the State Capitol building in Salem, the Oregon pioneer statue shimmers in the afternoon sunlight. Ulric Ellerhusen created this twenty-three-foot-tall figure, cast in bronze and finished in gold leaf. Despite being hollow, it weighs a whopping eight-and-a-half tons. The current building was built in 1938, replacing the previous capitol that was destroyed by a 1935 fire.

The 1898 Thomas Kay Woolen Mill is the central feature of Salem's Mission Mill Museum and a testament to early Salem enterprise. This structure replaced the 1890 woolen mill that was lost to fire in 1895. Visitors to the museum can learn about early-day fabric finishing, plus they can visit the 1841 Jason Lee House, the 1841 Methodist Parsonage, and the 1847 John D. Boone House. Missionary Jason Lee is attributed with founding Salem and Willamette University.

The lovely 1888 Italianate Benton County Courthouse in Corvallis is the oldest courthouse in Oregon still used for its original purpose. Holiday lights give this county landmark added appeal.

LEFT

Raymond Hunter's *Ballerina,* placed in Corvallis's Central Park in 1979, was the first public art along the city's Madison Avenue. Since then, a growing collection of art has sprung up in the alleys off Madison Avenue.

BELOW

Art at the Hult Center for the Performing Arts in Eugene is not limited to the performances, but also can be seen in the smallest detail of the center's architecture. More than 600 clay tiles, the "Catpaw Tiles" produced by Catpaw Pottery in Portland, lend a unique stripe to the Silva Concert Hall.

RIGHT

Traveling the backroads of the Willamette Valley reveals a host of rural images: barns, farmstands, cultivated fields, fruit and nut orchards, tractors, fences, and irrigation lines. Here, the rhythmic pattern of the irrigation wheels is complemented by rows of cultivated poppies.

ABOVE

Barns are endearing landmarks of our agricultural heritage, and the Gribble Barn in Clackamas County, south of Canby, is no exception. This huge barn was built in 1907 on the 640-acre Gribble homestead, but the barn's future is uncertain because its owners no longer own the property on which the barn sits. It has worn the "Flying Double-A" painted logo since 1986.

The Willamette Valley, the quested land of the Oregon Trail pioneer, produces an array of both fine food crops and ornamental flowers. Arriving just in time for Easter, colorful tulips dress the fields and display gardens at the Wooden Shoe Bulb Company, outside Woodburn.

In Yamhill County, the soaring barn at Bernards Farm attracts travelers with its seasonal produce and flowers. The Willamette Valley's growing conditions are ideal for all kinds of vegetables, berries, fruits, and nuts.

Yamhill County is wine country, and vineyards dress the hillsides. These are the vines of the Sokol Blosser Winery, in the county's Dundee Hills. This winery, and the Willamette Valley region, is known for its pinot noir.

LEFT

The Willamette Valley's mild climate and the rocky soils of its foothills create ideal growing conditions for the grape, giving rise to numerous vineyards and family wineries. Harvests typically come in late September or early October.

Sheep raising is an integral part of Linn County's rural profile, and Linn County is one of the leading sheep-raising counties in the state. The town of Scio hosts the annual Linn County Lamb and Wool Festival, as well as the Northwest Champion Sheep Dog Trial.

With the rising sun, a foggy mist lifts off the valley floor to give this Linn County oak an ethereal quality. The Willamette Valley enjoys a mild climate, with average annual rainfall of about forty inches, most of it arriving as winter rain.

At William L. Finley National Wildlife Refuge, south of Corvallis, wintering Canada geese lift off the lakes and valley floor in winged chaos, in response to feeding times or the overhead passage of a bald eagle. Together with Baskett Slough and Ankeny National Wildlife Refuges (west and south of Salem, respectively), this refuge makes up the Willamette Valley Wildlife Refuge Complex, which preserves traditional valley wintering grounds for the goose and other migrating birds.

The sun rises over the Columbia River Gorge. Over a 2,000-year period, 17,000 years ago, gargantuan Ice Age floods known as the Missoula Floods deluged the Columbia River with water, rock, and debris, gouging out this dramatic cleft between Oregon and Washington. The stunning beauty and recreational opportunity of the river gorge led to its receiving national scenic area distinction in 1986.

In the Columbia River Gorge National Scenic Area, Vista House sits atop Crown Point, 733 feet above the river. The octagonal structure was built between 1916 and 1918 as a memorial to the Oregon pioneer. Crown Point is a National Natural Landmark, the house a National Historic Place.

Italianate stonework complements the graceful curves of the Historic Columbia River Highway, which represents the vision of Samuel C. Hill and the feat of engineer Samuel C. Lancaster. It was the first scenic highway in America and is now a National Historic Place. The route seamlessly blends nature and construction at every turn for a rich visual experience.

More than a dozen major waterfalls grace the basalt cliffs on the Oregon side of the Columbia River Gorge. Wahclella Falls, also known as Tanner Falls, is among the stunning lineup and is reached via a one-mile trail. The tiered falls has an upper and lower drop, for a combined plummet in excess of sixty feet.

Autumn paints the bigleaf maples and vine maples around Multnomah Falls in the Columbia River Gorge National Scenic Area. Multnomah Falls is the number one natural attraction in the state and is the fourth-tallest falls in the nation, spilling a combined 620 feet in two stages.

Balsamroot decorates this terrace vantage at Tom McCall Preserve in the Columbia River Gorge National Scenic Area. Within the gorge, some 1,250 of the 4,000 native Oregon plants find habitat. Variations in soil, sun, water, and temperature between elevations and between east-west locations give rise to this abundance. The spring bloom runs from mid-March through June.

Sturgeon fishing poles stand at attention in front of Bonneville Dam. Bonneville is one of a series of dams harnessing the power of the mighty Columbia River. The dam was a major national project of the Depression Era, bringing jobs, power, and pride to the Pacific Northwest.

Windsurfers shoot across the Columbia River at Mayer State Park. Stiff winds are a signature of the Columbia River Gorge, the result of pressure differences on the east and west sides of the Cascades. The Gorge, as the only gap in the mountains, works as a wind tunnel.

Grain elevators, historic and new, are the skyscrapers of farm country. This grain elevator sits near the Deschutes River in Maupin. The loess soil of the Columbia Plateau is ideal for wheat growing, and large commercial wheat fields roll across this otherwise vacant expanse.

Hood River County, centrally located along the Columbia River Gorge, is known for its fruit growing: cherries, apples, peaches, and pears. Springtime finds this pear orchard in full bloom. Hood River County is the nation's leading producer of Anjou pears.

In Mount Hood National Forest, the Old Salmon River Trail parallels the bank of the Salmon Wild and Scenic River and threads through a classic Cascade Mountains forest of Douglas fir and western hemlock. Thick mosses, sword ferns, Oregon grapes, and a host of other flora bring shape, texture, and all shades of green to the forest floor.

A gallery of ten major waterfalls graces Silver Creek Canyon in Silver Falls State Park, east of Salem. Here, the plummeting waters of ninety-three-foot Lower South Falls fan the leaves of a bigleaf maple. The Trail of Ten Falls carries hikers behind this watery curtain for an unusual look at the canyon and the waterfall.

ABOVE

At 11,235 feet, Mount Hood is the highest peak in Oregon and the fourth-tallest Cascade Mountains volcano. (Washington's Mount Rainier is the tallest at 14,411 feet.) Here, Mount Hood is seen in her snowy finery from the White Wild and Scenic River.

RIGHT

Timberline Lodge, a national historic landmark, has a construction of rough stone masonry and heavy timbers. It sits near the 6,000-foot elevation of Mount Hood (tree line) and receives a hearty snowfall. Fully restored, the lodge continues to offer overnight lodging and provide access to the mountain's winter and summer ski area and the forty-mile Timberline Trail.

This carving adorns the front entry door to Timberline Lodge. The lodge was built during the Depression using natural building materials, and it showcases the fine masonry, woodwork, and carvings of master craftsmen.

Mount Jefferson peeks over the shoulder of Timberline Lodge in this view looking south from the Timberline Trail on Mount Hood. The Timberline Trail encircles Mount Hood at the 6,000-foot elevation, and popular climbing routes branch from it.

Dawn's blue light washes over the canoes docked at rustic Olallie Lake Resort in Olallie Lake Scenic Area. The 11,000-acre scenic area sits along the north-central Cascade Crest in Mount Hood National Forest. It is noted for its necklace of lakes and ponds, its huckleberries (*olallie*), and its bumpy cinder butte skyline.

LEFT

A pair of chipmunks share a tasty morsel at Olallie Lake Scenic Area in Mount Hood National Forest. The body stripes of chipmunks extend to their noses. Golden-mantled ground squirrels, which are commonly mistaken for chipmunks, are similarly striped but lack facial striping.

ABOVE

This white-headed woodpecker chose a ponderosa pine along the Metolius Wild and Scenic River for its nest. The Metolius River, in Deschutes National Forest northwest of Sisters, is one of the most scenic rivers in the Pacific Northwest. Kingfishers, ospreys, herons, flickers, and western tanagers are commonly seen along the river—as are hip-wader-wearing anglers enjoying the blue-ribbon fly-fishing waters.

Mount Jefferson overlooks the high meadow, forest, and lake basin of Hunts Cove in Mount Jefferson Wilderness. Mount Jefferson is the second-tallest peak in the state at 10,495 feet. Lewis and Clark first sighted the mountain from the Willamette River mouth in March 1806. They named the volcano in honor of President Thomas Jefferson, who commissioned the expedition.

ABOVE

Flowing along Oregon Highway 58 east of Eugene, Salt Creek is a rather understated creek in the Willamette National Forest, with one exception: the 286-foot columnar plunge of Salt Creek Falls. This is the second-tallest falls in the state and the most powerful spill in southern Oregon, averaging 50,000 gallons per minute. A popular viewing turnout with short trails offers falls viewing.

OPPOSITE

Western Oregon holds a wealth of waterfall treasures. Marion Falls spills in Mount Jefferson Wilderness downstream from Marion Lake, a popular hiking destination. Winter transforms the watery tresses with snow, ice, and frost but limits waterfall access to determined and sure-footed travelers only.

RIGHT

A wintry brine of ice and snow holds a fast grip on these conifers near Timberline Lodge on Mount Hood. Mount Hood receives an average annual snowfall of 430 inches. Winter is a season of great beauty, but it can also be brutal, with fierce winds creating whiteout conditions.

Scout Lake, a high-country lake in Mount Jefferson Wilderness, provides this view of Mount Jefferson and its watery double. Mount Jefferson Wilderness encompasses more than 111,000 acres within Willamette National Forest and includes more than 150 lakes.

RIGHT

In Oregon, vine maples undergo some of the most brilliant fall color changes. Typically, the vine maple is a midstory shrub that bridges the view between the treetops and the forest floor, but it also finds suitable habitat growing out in the open on lava flows.

BELOW

This mountain finder sits atop Dee Wright Observatory, located southwest of Sisters along the McKenzie Pass–Santiam Pass National Scenic Byway. Composing the neighborhood are the volcanic features of the Mount Jefferson, Mount Washington, and Three Sisters Wilderness Areas. The observatory, built of lava, sits atop a 1,500-year-old lava flow.

Northwest of Sisters in Deschutes National Forest, the Metolius River emerges from springs deep beneath Black Butte. The river captivates with its icy blue trenches and black satin flows, its wildflower islands, and wild trout.

Built in 1938, Goodpasture Bridge on the Lower McKenzie River is one of the most photographed covered bridges in Oregon. At 165 feet long, it is the state's second-longest covered-bridge span, after the 180-foot-long Office Bridge in Westfir. The distinguishing characteristic of the Goodpasture Bridge is the ten gothic-style windows on each side.

In its search for a share of state tourism dollars after the decline of the timber industry, Sisters hit the mark with its 1880s frontier image. Its boardwalks bustle year-round with shoppers. The town's backdrop of the Three Sisters Mountains doesn't hurt either.

Off U.S. Highway 97 between Bend and Redmond, Petersen Rock Garden offers a quirky little roadside stop. Rasmus Petersen was a farmer with an extensive rock collection and an even greater imagination, and the garden is the product of the two colliding. Intricately detailed cottages, bold expressions of patriotism, castles, and the fantastic—all composed of painstakingly placed stones—dress the four-acre site.

Tucked away in Deschutes County near Deschutes Junction (north of Bend), The Funny Farm offers an eclectic and offbeat display of art made from recycled and reused materials. Bowling-ball gardens and rainbow roofs take the place of rose bushes and white picket fences, and big pink heads fit right in.

Public art dots the Bend landscape. This piece, *Sunrise Spirit Column* by David Govedare, is located at the center of the Mount Washington Roundabout (a traffic-control circle). Constructed of basalt, granite, steel, and copper, the art is intended to inspire positive energy in the world.

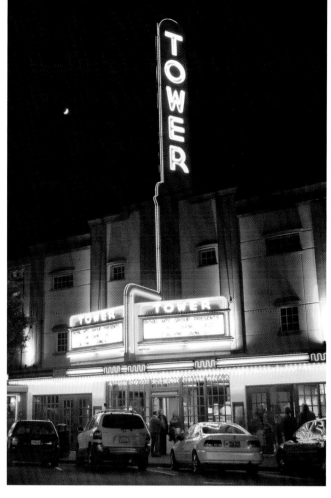

ABOVE

Summer was made for outdoor concerts, such as this one at the Les Schwab Amphitheater in Bend's Old Mill District. Sun hats, blankets, lawn chairs, cool drinks, and tapping toes are the order of the day.

ABOVE

Going to the picture show became an American institution in the first half of the twentieth century, and nearly every town of suitable size had its marquee theater, its picture palace. The Tower Theater is Bend's.

LEFT

The carnival, with dizzying lights and rides, contributes to the festive atmosphere at Boatnik, which takes place at Riverside Park in Grants Pass. This Memorial Day celebration includes a variety of boat races, highlighted by the whitewater hydroplane races.

A city landmark, the fully restored Ashland Springs Hotel offers bygone elegance with contemporary comfort. Built in 1925, it was first called the Lithia Hotel and later the Mark Antony. The hotel is on the National Register of Historic Places.

Earthstar, also known as the Ashland Fairy, is a familiar, and memorable, fixture at the Artisans Market in Ashland. She sells the props that let little girls become fairy princesses. Oregon has a large arts and crafts community, and street vending is a popular way to link crafters to potential buyers.

Valley oaks are a signature of the Bureau of Land Management's North Bank Habitat Management Area, northeast of Roseburg. This 6,500-acre parcel was acquired to provide habitat for the Columbian whitetail deer. Wild turkeys also favor the spot.

LEFT

Gristmills, such as the Butte Creek Mill in Eagle Point, were the centerpieces of early settlement. This interior display at the Butte Creek Mill represents the owner's personal collection of early food packaging. The mill is still operational, with a full lineup of fresh-milled flours and grain products.

ABOVE

Historic Jacksonville, southern Oregon's first town, owes its start to gold, discovered in 1851. By the following year, Jacksonville was a thriving boomtown with saloons, shops, gambling halls, and a bank. Mercantiles were at the center of commerce, supplying flour, foodstuffs, and hardware to the miners. Today's Jacksonville Mercantile, in the 1861 Warehouse Building, is a purveyor of fine specialty foods.

In 1872, Modoc leader Captain Jack rebelled against a military order to send his people to the Klamath Indian Reservation—the home of their historic enemy. With a ragtag band of fifty-two Modocs, he held off the cavalry for five months at what is now Lava Beds National Monument in Northern California. Their heroic resistance ended at Fort Klamath, Oregon, with the trial and execution of Captain Jack and three others. Simple markers note their graves at today's Fort Klamath Historic Site.

When the Southern Oregon Historical Society welcomes the public to events at its Historic Hanley Farm, outside Medford, the Belgian workhorses are a popular attraction. The horses draw the wagons that take visitors around the farm. Mules, llamas, alpacas, and miniature horses may also be seen.

At Hanley Farm, Southern Oregon Historical Society members demonstrate threshing as it was done at the turn of the twentieth century. Here, they shock, gather, thresh, bag, and bale the summer grain in front of one of the property's two barns.

At the Steele Visitor Center in Crater Lake National Park, the American flag flies against a wintry backdrop. Crater Lake averages 533 inches of snow per year. The snow begins to accumulate in October and doesn't start to melt until June.

Winter's grasp on this small visitor center at Crater Lake National Park is unflinching. Here, winter has a way of declaring its own wilderness, with limited visibility and access. But for snowshoers and cross-country skiers, the scenery is spellbinding.

Crater Lake traces its origin to the cataclysmic eruptions 7,700 years ago of the ancient volcano Mount Mazama. This now-dormant volcano is part of the chain of volcanoes stretched along the Cascade Crest from Mount Garibaldi (near Vancouver, British Columbia) to Mount Lassen (in California). Parasitic cones on Mazama's flanks created Mount Scott (shown here) and Hillman Peak.

Another year of winter snow takes its toll on this broken-down shack in Deadwood Prairie in the Rogue River National Forest. No doubt, time and the elements will eventually win out, and this piece of history will fade into the landscape.

Hanging Rock, a ridgeline outcrop along the Panther Ridge Trail in Siskiyou National Forest, juts out over the Wild Rogue Wilderness. It serves up views and is itself a striking image. Violet-green swallows dart from crannies below the dome.

In the Siskiyou Mountains, carnivorous pitcher plants thrive alongside Lower Vulcan Lake within the Kalmiopsis Wilderness. Protected since 1946, the now 180,000-acre Kalmiopsis Wilderness is noted for its rugged terrain and rare botanics. An estimated 2,000 flowering plants dot the wilderness landscape, including several rare and endangered species that raise their heads here and nowhere else.

LEFT

The native wild azalea is a decorative understory or midstory shrub adorning the forests and shores of southwestern Oregon. Within its range, the town of Brookings is home to the thirty-three-acre Azalea Park. Since 1939, the town has hosted the annual Azalea Festival.

LEFT

The Siskiyou iris, yellow to pale yellow in color, has a more limited range than its purple counterpart, the Douglas iris. Its growth is limited to the Siskiyou Mountains of southwest Oregon and to the adjoining northern extreme of California.

Buttercups herald spring in the expansive meadow flat of Sparks Lake, along Cascade Lakes Scenic Byway southwest of Bend. Sparks Lake is a big shallow lake popularized by Oregon photographer laureate Ray Atkeson. A short trail created in Atkeson's honor visits one of his favorite Oregon vantages, pairing Sparks Lake and South Sister.

Balsamroots, members of the sunflower tribe, dot color to the arid slopes of the Deschutes River canyon. The Deschutes Wild and Scenic River is a popular recreational waterway with premier trout and steelhead fishing, boating, and whitewater rafting. Hiking trails and scenic byways provide still other means of enjoying the river.

The Deschutes Wild and Scenic River is one of the state's most popular whitewater rivers; Class III and IV rapids agitate the lower river. Rapids bearing such colorful names as Boxcar, Rollercoaster, Elevator, Trestle, and Wreck heighten excitement before the water even hits you.

Peter Skene Ogden State Park, named for an early-day trapper and explorer, offers a striking overlook of the Crooked River in central Oregon. The river has carved out an impressively deep, vertical-walled canyon through the thick basalt.

OPPOSITE
The golden-red rhyolite-ash cliffs and spires of Smith Rock rise above the aptly named Crooked River at Smith Rock State Park near Terrebonne, north of Redmond. This 640-acre, high-desert park is a world-renowned climbing park. Smith Summit rises 800 feet above the Crooked River, and eagles nest on the high rock ledges.

LEFT
Junipers, pines, sagebrush, rabbitbrush, and native grasses vegetate the Crooked River canyon at Smith Rock State Park. Here, a juniper stands in dark silhouette against Smith Rock, which has turned golden under the morning light.

A hallmark of Smith Rock State Park is the pull-apart spire descriptively named Monkey Face. The park's geology is the product of two great forces: volcanism and erosion.

ABOVE

Morning Glory Wall, The Dihedrals, The Christian Brothers, and Monkey Face hold some of the most popular climbs at Smith Rock State Park, but hundreds of routes are available. This climber is testing his mettle on Monkey Face.

ABOVE

A solitary canoeist enjoys peaceful pursuits on the Upper Klamath Lake Canoe Trail at sunrise. This popular canoe route in Upper Klamath National Wildlife Refuge takes paddlers past open water and vegetated marsh. The quiet approach of the canoe increases the number of wildlife sightings and typically allows for closer viewing.

LEFT

Below southern Oregon's Abert Rim, orange-colored lichen paints the volcanic rock scatter along Lake Abert. On other rocks, Indian petroglyphs record early travel here. The broad, glassy lake hosts great numbers of waterfowl.

At Christmas Valley, sagebrush and rabbitbrush stretch out across the flat expanse as far as the eye can see. This area was once a prehistoric inland sea, which accounts for the flatness. An estimated 30,000 mule deer winter in the area.

Stage routes crisscrossed the western frontier in the nineteenth century, bringing communities together; depicted here is Camp Creek Stage Stop in Crook County. Remnants of the past dot the wide-open spaces of central and eastern Oregon, each with a story to tell.

The golden light of late day bathes the dusty cattle as they move between grazing areas. Cattle ranching is a primary enterprise in southern and eastern Oregon, where the frontier is alive and well.

Turkey vultures roost on a ponderosa pine snag near Blue Sky at Hart Mountain National Antelope Refuge. These scavengers often carry a negative reputation, but they play a vital role in the overall health of the environment. They achieve a noble bearing when soaring upon the thermals.

Steens Mountain, south of Burns in southeastern Oregon, is the largest fault-block mountain in North America. It stretches out thirty miles long and shoots up a vertical mile from the Alvord Desert. East Rim Overlook, near the mountain summit, provides a dizzying look down the mountain's abrupt drop and across the sweeping desert.

On the upper reaches of Steens Mountain, the cobalt water of Wildhorse Lake benefits wildlife and shines like a looking glass, reflecting the rugged neighborhood.

Steens Mountain has a big vertical relief, rising from a 4,100-foot elevation at the high-desert floor to the 9,700-foot summit. This elevation change creates distinct vegetation zones as you move up the mountain: sagebrush, juniper, aspen, upland prairies, and tortured subalpine tundra. Mountain mahogany, shown here at sunset, dots the upland, favoring steep rocky locations in the 6,000- to 8,000-foot-elevation range.

This wildflower meadow lies along Steens Mountain National Back Country Byway, the highest climbing road in Oregon, topping out at 9,700 feet. On the high-desert mountain, the summer bloom arrives late and hurries to its conclusion before the first snow flies.

The Donner und Blitzen River sheets over rocks as it flows past the Riddle Brothers Ranch National Historic District in Steens Mountain Recreation Area. The Riddle Brothers operated a horse and cattle ranch in the Little Blitzen Canyon in the 1900s, and desert water sources were vital to their operation.

In the lonesome outback southeast of Burns, the Peter French Round Barn, now a state park, is one of the far-flung structures of the P Ranch cattle empire of the late 1800s. The barn's innovative round design allowed cowboys to exercise horses during the chilly eastern Oregon winters in an obstacle-free arena.

Deer briefly pause in alert while browsing in the deep grasses at Malheur National Wildlife Refuge. Considered one of the ten best birding spots in the nation, Malheur National Wildlife Refuge covers an impressive 187,000 acres and houses more than 320 bird species and nearly 60 mammal species.

A basic characteristic of Oregon's Basin and Range lakes is the rise and fall of the lake-water levels. This fluctuation is critical to keeping the waters nutrient rich and is what allows the lakes to support great numbers of migrating birds. During a dry cycle on Harney Lake, a tile-like surface of cracked mud provides little clue to the thriving lake that exists in wet years.

ABOVE

A bighorn sheep stands in silhouette among the high-rise cliffs of Juniper Gulch in the Leslie Gulch Area of southeast Oregon (south of Vale). The Leslie Gulch Area is an 11,653-acre Bureau of Land Management Area of Critical Environmental Concern. The volcanic tuff of the area's canyons is a product of two eruptions more than fifteen million years ago.

ABOVE

A lonesome cabin sits alongside the Imnaha Wild and Scenic River in Hells Canyon National Recreation Area. Stalwart pioneers tried to eke out existences even in the state's harshest and most remote reaches.

Oregon has some of the finest fishing rivers in the nation. This angler tries her luck on the clear waters of the Imnaha Wild and Scenic River in Hells Canyon National Recreation Area.

ABOVE

Stud Creek Trail serves up this view of the Snake Wild and Scenic River in Hells Canyon National Recreation Area. The Snake River carved out Hells Canyon, the deepest river gorge in North America. The gorge measures an impressive one-and-a-half miles deep and has an average width of ten miles.

LEFT

Named for its ponderous size, the ponderosa pine shapes one of the climax forests east of the Cascades. The golden-orange color of the trunk at maturity suggests the tree's nickname, "yellow-belly." These pines dress the view of Elkhorn Crest in Wallowa-Whitman National Forest in northeastern Oregon.

Steins Pillar, reached by a hiking trail in Ochoco National Forest, is a massive 350-foot, free-standing, pinkish monolith, streaked black with desert varnish at its crown. It rises out of its neighborhood with the surprise of a child's first popup book.

In the Elkhorn Mountains, the aptly named Gunsight Mountain keeps sentinel over Anthony Lake, a popular recreational lake in eastern Oregon. The rugged Elkhorn Mountains are remote enough for mountain goats, but more common sightings are Clark's nutcrackers and gray jays. Elk frequent the pocket meadows below the crest.

RIGHT

Northeast Oregon's Wallowa Valley is home to several historic and beautiful barns, including the Crossed Sabers Ranch round barn, located near Hells Canyon National Scenic Byway in the shadow of the Wallowa Mountains. In addition to its ranching heritage, the Wallowa Valley is also the historical home of Chief Joseph and the Nez Perce Indians.

ABOVE

Backroads travel throughout the state brings many reminders of bygone days. This picturesque old homestead in Sherman County was discovered off the Journey Through Time Scenic Byway.

OPPOSITE

Painted Hills Trail provides this overlook of the badlands at the Painted Hills Unit of John Day Fossil Beds National Monument, northwest of Mitchell. The Clarno Unit, near Fossil, and the Sheep Rock Unit, near Dayville, complete the monument threesome. Terraced palisades, fluted cliffs, and prehistoric fossils are their offerings.

BELOW

Red, buff, gold, and black bands paint the rumpled badlands at the Painted Hills Unit. Periods of rain intensify the color.

117

ABOVE

This elder in full regalia awaits the start of the
Pi-Ume-Sha Treaty Days parade at the Warm Springs
Indian Reservation in central Oregon. Treaty Days,
celebrated each June, commemorates the 1855 treaty
that confirmed the rights of the central Oregon tribes to
the Warm Springs Indian Reservation. It also confirmed
their rights to fish, hunt, and gather on traditional sites.

ABOVE

Children in customary tribal garb join in the celebration
of the Pi-Ume-Sha Treaty Days. A powwow, complete with
Grand Entrance, a parade, and an endurance horse race
are part of the celebration.

Cattle outnumber people in remote eastern Oregon, and roundups, cattle drives, and brandings are common sights. From the time the lands east of the Cascades were first opened to settlement, ranching has played a vital role here.

ABOVE

Rodeos are a rite of summer in the rural counties of
the state. Here, horses, riders, and livestock fly out of the
chute at the Haines Rodeo in eastern Oregon.

BELOW

Youngsters get in on the action, as well, at junior rodeos. Undersized heroes in oversized hats, wielding oversized ropes, are sure to win over audiences. This little contender awaits his turn at the Hells Canyon Junior Rodeo in Halfway.

A dozen life-size bronze statues adorn the streets of Joseph, nestled in the Wallowa Mountains. Subjects include horses, wildlife, Native Americans, cowboys, and a barefoot girl on a garden path. The town strikes a working balance between art and specialty shops and pickup trucks and cowboy boots.

The celebrated Geiser Grand Hotel, built in 1889, recalls Baker City's golden past and continues to dazzle guests with old-time elegance. The Geiser family acquired their wealth in the area gold mines. In its heyday, this hotel offered the finest accommodations between Salt Lake City and Seattle.

The card pinned to the mannequin reads:

Mr. Johnnie Zeph — one of the oldest pioneers, he arrived in Grant County in 1863. He was in charge of the Good Templar's Hall and was the doorman at the lodge meetings. When members arrived, he shouted out, "Admit the brother if he is duly sober."

Oregon's many small historical museums are untapped treasures. Inside the Grant County Historical Museum in Canyon City, Joaquin Miller's inkwells, the skulls of the first two men hanged in town, a tin of Dixie Queen tobacco, and a ship carved by a jailhouse inmate may detain eyes. The seated mannequin represents Johnnie Zeph, one of the county's earliest pioneers. Zeph arrived here in 1863.

LEFT

Kam Wah Chung State Park preserves this former Chinese apothecary and store in the town of John Day, in the heart of eastern Oregon cowboy country. Doc Hay, a respected Chinese pulsologist and herbalist, treated both white and Chinese patients. Upon Hay's death in 1948, the shop's doors closed, and nothing was disturbed until the museum opened in 1978. This unique time capsule holds 500 herbs, canned goods, bootleg whiskey, and religious artifacts.

ABOVE

In Haines, north of Baker City, a collection of historic area cabins has been brought together in the 1880s Park. Among them is the oldest wooden structure in Baker County, the Chandler Cabin. This one-room home is furnished in the style of the 1880s.

In the mid-1800s, the grueling 2,000-mile overland route of the Oregon Trail brought emigrants west to the promise of new lives in fertile lands. This is the entrance sign to the Oregon Trail Interpretive Park at the trail's Blue Mountain Crossing, near La Grande. Worn into the earth are remnant wagon ruts.

Windmills are iconic western images. The simple devices brought the all-important water from the ground to the surface for watering livestock. This windmill is found in Sherman County, along the Journey Through Time Scenic Byway.

About the Author

George Ostertag has been exploring Oregon and the Pacific Northwest for more than twenty years, uncovering the region's prized haunts and raptures. As a professional nature and travel photographer, he has worked independently and in collaboration with his author-wife, Rhonda, to produce numerous books and articles. They settled in the Northwest for its outdoor ethic and its great diversity: mountains, ocean, deserts, valleys, rural heartlands, and cutting-edge cities. With such variety, Ostertag's shutter is seldom still. He is out in all kinds of weather and up before the first break of light.

George has collaborated on nearly twenty guidebooks and hundreds of articles. His photography commonly pops up on calendar pages and postcard racks. His most recent title is Voyageur Press's *Backroads of Oregon* (2005).